ANIMAL STATS

AMAZING ANIMALS

SIMON ABBOTT

Enslow PUBLISHING

Published in 2027 by Enslow Publishing, LLC
2544 Clinton Street
Buffalo, NY 14224

First published in Great Britain in 2025 by Wayland

Printed in China

CPSIA compliance information: Batch #QS27ENS: For further information contact Enslow Publishing LLC, New York, New York at 1-800-398-2504.

Please visit our website, www.enslowpublishing.com. For a free color catalog of all our high-quality books, call toll free 1-800-398-2504 or fax 1-877-980-4454.

Cataloging-in-Publication Data

Names: Abbott, Simon, 1967-.
Title: Amazing animals / Simon Abbott.
Description: Buffalo, NY : Enslow Publishing, 2027. |
Series: Animal stats | Includes glossary.
Identifiers: ISBN 9781978549265 (pbk.) | ISBN 9781978549272 (library bound) |
ISBN 9781978549289 (ebook)
Subjects: LCSH: Animals--Juvenile literature.
Classification: LCC QL49.A34 2027 | DDC 590--dc23

Find us on

CONTENTS

STEP INTO THE INCREDIBLE WORLD OF *ANIMAL STATS*!

Prepare to be amazed as you learn about the **6,000** species of mammals, **10,000** types of reptiles, and **11,000** different birds that share our planet with **33,000** types of fish, over **8,000** different amphibians, and **1 million** species of insects!

These fascinating creatures have adapted to survive in every corner of the globe – from the highest mountain peaks to the deepest underground burrows.

They thrive in the scorching heat of deserts and brave freezing temperatures on icebergs.

Discover the smartest specimens, the speediest sprinters, the strongest superstars, and the hefty heavyweights who top the scales!

TURN THE PAGE AND EMBARK ON AN EXCITING ANIMAL ADVENTURE LIKE NO OTHER!

A STEP BACK IN TIME

Animals have been walking, running, jumping, climbing, hopping, and swinging around planet Earth for over **210 million** years.

The oldest mammal we know of is **Brasilodon.** This tiny shrew-like specimen was no larger than a smartphone and weighed the same as a tennis ball.

All mammals, including you, have evolved from creatures who survived the devastating dinosaur extinction.

PAW-FECT PETS!

Around **12,000-14,000** years ago, people realized that wolf cubs could be trained. Wolves are the distant ancestor of all modern-day dogs.

So, what makes a mammal, and what list of requirements does a reptile have? Let's see if this helps:

MAMMAL ESSENTIALS

1. They are warm-blooded
2. They are **endothermic** (they can regulate their heat from inside their bodies)
3. They feed their young with milk
4. They have a bony skeleton
5. Their brain is more developed than other animals' brains
6. They breathe air

REPTILE REQUIREMENTS

1. They are cold-blooded
2. They are **ectothermic** (they rely on their environment for heat)
3. Most reptiles lay eggs on land
4. They have scaly bodies instead of fur or feathers
5. All reptiles have a backbone
6. They breathe air too!

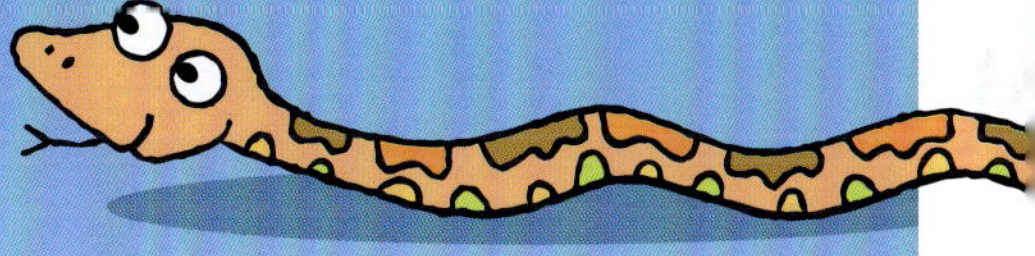

BIRD REQUIREMENTS

1. They are warm-blooded
2. They are **endothermic**
3. Birds lay eggs
4. They have feathers instead of fur or scales
5. Birds have beaks instead of teeth
6. They are vertebrates, so have a bony skeleton

FEATHERY FACTS!!

Around **150 million** years ago, birds descended from a group of meat-eating dinosaurs called **theropods**. This makes them more closely related to reptiles than mammals.

HOME SWEET HOME

Part of the animals' success story is their ability to adapt to almost any environment, or habitat.

There are **10** main types of land habitat on our planet. Let's see them all.

HABITAT	CONDITIONS	WHO LIVES THERE?
Mountains (e.g. Himalayas)	Cold and windy weather with little to eat 	Snow leopards, bighorn sheep, mountain hares, mountain goats, golden eagles, vultures, lizards
Savanna (e.g. Tropical Africa)	Grasslands, with hot and dry weather and seasons of heavy rainfall of up to 40 inches (1 m) per year	African elephants, giraffes, lions, meerkats, gazelles, zebras, ostriches, flamingos, Nile crocodiles 
Coniferous Forests (Found in Canada, Alaska, Scandinavia)	Cold and dry in the winter, warm and moist in the short summer 	Moose, beavers, wolves, squirrels, reindeer, woodpeckers, owls, salamanders, garter snakes
Deciduous Forest (Found in Europe, Japan, China, North America)	Mild and wet. Trees grow quickly in the summer and lose their leaves in the winter	Rabbits, foxes, bears, badgers, deer, hawks, jays, turtles, frogs 
Polar Ice Caps (North and South Poles)	Coldest temperatures on Earth, with freezing ice and snow	Seals, polar bears, Arctic foxes, penguins, puffins, Arctic terns 

Antarctica is the coldest continent on Earth, with an average temperature of -70.6°F (-57°C)

HABITAT	CONDITIONS	WHO LIVES THERE?
Tropical Rainforest (Near the equator - an imaginary line around the middle of Earth)	Hot and wet. The Amazon rainforest averages **5 to 10 inches (13 to 25 cm)** of rain per year. Plants grow all year round	Giant otters, jaguars, howler monkeys, macaws, hornbills, harpy eagles, caimans, iguanas
Hot Deserts (Found in Africa, Australia, Mexico, Southwest USA)	Hot and dry with very little plant life	Camels, fennec foxes, jerboas, prairie dogs, ospreys, desert larks, bearded dragons, geckos
Tundra (Below the ice caps in North America, Europe, and Siberia)	Frozen solid for much of the year, with ice thawing slightly in spring and summer	Arctic hares, lemmings, polar bears, yaks, walruses, snowy owls, king eiders
Temperate Grassland (Open grassy plains in Argentina, Australia, and North America)	Seasonal weather including tornados, blizzards, drought, and occasional fires	Bison, wild horses, jack rabbits, ibis, lapwings, leopard tortoises, black mamba snakes
Mediterranean (Spain, Greece, Turkey, Syria, North Africa)	Hot, but with more rainfall than desert regions	Iberian lynx, Barbary apes, mouflon sheep, Spanish imperial eagles, storks, pelicans, rock lizards, geckos

The Sahara is the hottest and driest desert on Earth, with an average rainfall of 3 inches (76 mm) and temperatures over 122°F (50°C)

BRANCHING OUT

The Amazon rainforest is a whopping **2.6 million square miles** (6.7million km^2) of wonder, stretching through eight South American countries.
In fact, you could fit the whole of India or **28** United Kingdoms inside it!

But why is it such a big deal? Well, with its warm and humid climate, the rainforest ia a paradise for plants that thrive all year round. And where there are plants, there is animal life - just take a look at the **427** species of mammals that live there! These incredible creatures share the rainforest with **40,000** plant species, **1,300** bird varieties, **3,000** types of fish, and an incredible **2.5 million** insect specimens.

In fact, the Amazon rainforest is home to **10%** of all the known wildlife species on Earth.

The rainforest can be divided into **four** different layers:

EMERGENT

The top layer, with treetops as high as **200 feet (60 m)**. You can spot harpy eagles, bats and butterflies here.

CANOPY

A deep layer, formed by a dense network of branches and leaves. Sloths, toucans, and red-eyed tree frogs live here.

UNDERSTORY

A layer of younger and shorter trees, which grow under the canopy. Geckos, green mamba snakes, and boa constrictors call this home.

FOREST FLOOR

A shaded area, where few plants can grow. You'll find tapirs, armadillos, jaguars, and okapis here.

Let's speed things up a little, with the race to become the "fastest animal in the Amazon rainforest." After a close competition, the result is a tie!

Both the **jaguar** and **harpy eagle** reach a top speed of

50 miles per hour (80 km/h)!

Grab the scales and find the tape measure. Let's discover which other record-breaking rainforest inhabitants deserve a place in the hall of fame.

First up is the Amazonian manatee. Weighing in at almost **half a ton** and growing up to **9 feet** (2.8 m) long. This colossal creature is longer than your bed, which makes it the largest mammal in the Amazon rainforest.

The **capybara** is the world's largest rodent.

It can weigh as much as **110 pounds** (50 kg) which is twice as heavy as a dalmatian. And get this – it's a superstar swimmer with webbed feet for splashing around in the Amazon river!

Cover your ears – it's time to reveal the Amazon's noisiest animal. Congratulations to the **howler monkey!** This mammal has one of the loudest roars in the animal kingdom.

Their ear-splitting whoops and barks can be heard **3 miles** (5 km) away, as they sound the alarm or intimidate other monkeys who have tip-toed into their territory.

RAINFOREST RACKET

At **140 decibels,** the howler monkey's shout is as loud as a jet engine (and even louder than a pneumatic drill!).

The "number-one hunter" award goes to the fast and furious **harpy eagle.**

This bird boasts a wingspan of **6.5 feet** (2 m), which allows it to glide across the rainforest like a silent assassin.

A harpy eagle's laser-like vision is **eight times** stronger than a human's, and once it locks on to its prey, it grips on with talons as long as

5 inches

Nothing is off-limits – their targets include sloths, monkeys, macaws, snakes, and even baby deer.

If you're planning a visit to the Amazon rainforest, it might be worth keeping this chart handy. Here's a rundown of the animals you might want to keep at arm's length. **(Don't say we didn't warn you!)**

5TH MOST DEADLY! — ELECTRIC EEL

These slippery specimens can release an electrical charge of up to **860** volts. Ouch!

GREEN ANACONDA — 4TH MOST DEADLY!

The good news is that these snakes aren't venomous.

The bad news is that they use their superstrong muscles to squeeze their prey to death. Gulp!

3RD MOST DEADLY!

JAGUAR

Their name comes from the word "**yaguar**," which means "he who kills with one leap."

Need I say more?

PIRANHA

2ND MOST DEADLY!

These fish have interlocking upper and lower razor-sharp teeth, which makes them super-efficient meat slicers.

Yikes!

1ST THE RAINFOREST'S DEADLIEST ANIMAL!

POISON DART FROG

These reptiles are brightly colored so they should be easy to spot. However, some species carry enough venom to kill **10** humans. Eeek!

THE DUSTY DESERT

Did you know that about **one-third** of Earth's land surface is covered by deserts? And it's not just hot and sandy places - even **Antarctica** can be considered a desert! But what actually makes a desert? Well, it's a place that loses more water through evaporation than it gets from rainfall.

Some deserts, like the **Atacama Desert** in Chile, get as little as **0.04 inch** (1 mm) of rain per year.

That's less than the width of a spaghetti strand!

LET'S LOOK AT SOME DESERT DATA:

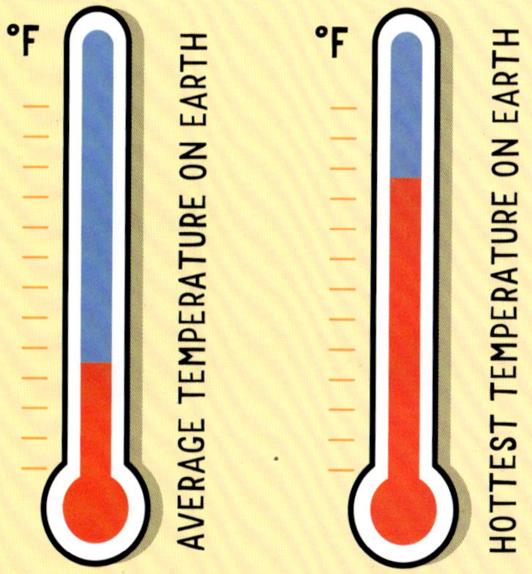

The hottest place on Earth is the **Lut Desert** in Iran. Temperatures of **159°F** (70.7°C) have been recorded here.

To put it into context, the average temperature on Earth is **59°F** (15°C).

The largest desert on Earth is the continent of **Antarctica.**

It covers an area of **5.5 million square miles** (14.2 million km²) - that's **one-tenth** of Earth's land area!

The largest hot desert is the **Sahara.**

At **3.6 million square miles** (9.4 million km²), it's about the size of the United States.

Despite the barren landscape and **122°F** (50°C) heat, the Sahara Desert is home to **2.5 million** people, **70** mammal species, **90** types of bird, **100** reptile varieties, and a huge number of insects.

Let's get the low-down on the scorching desert survivors.
How do they adapt to some of the harshest conditions on Earth?

CAMELS

Camels have a unique way of storing **fat** in their humps, which helps them survive in harsh conditions by providing energy and keeping their body temperature the same.

A camel can also remove **water vapor** from the air they breathe and absorb it into their body.

With their tough lips and tongue, and a mouth lined with firm bumps, called **papillae,** camels can munch away on thorny desert plants without harming themselves.

They can reduce water loss, as their **urine** is thick and syrupy, and their **poops** are dry. (In fact, they can even be used as firelighters!)

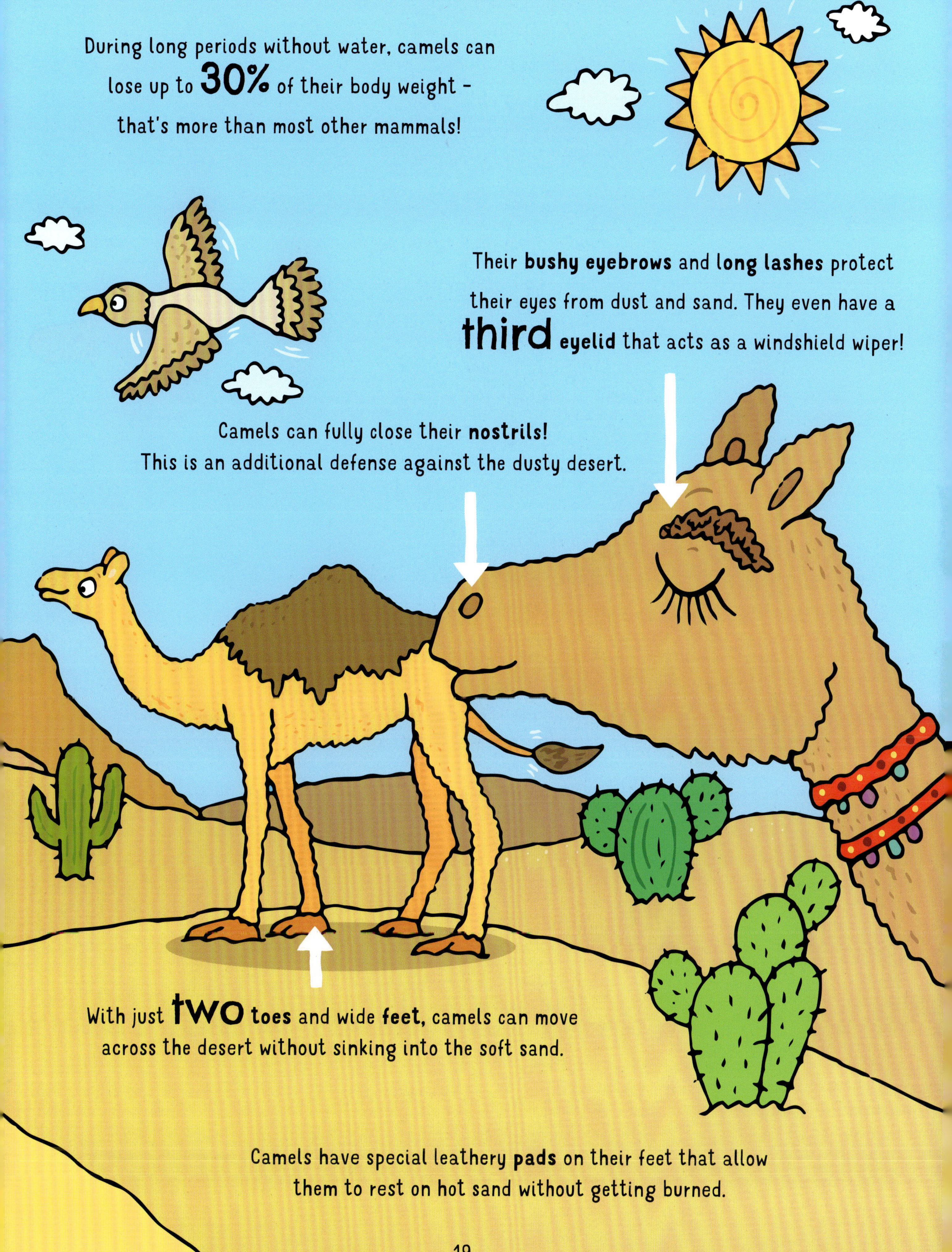

During long periods without water, camels can lose up to **30%** of their body weight – that's more than most other mammals!

Their **bushy eyebrows** and **long lashes** protect their eyes from dust and sand. They even have a **third eyelid** that acts as a windshield wiper!

Camels can fully close their **nostrils!** This is an additional defense against the dusty desert.

With just **two toes** and wide **feet,** camels can move across the desert without sinking into the soft sand.

Camels have special leathery **pads** on their feet that allow them to rest on hot sand without getting burned.

PRONGHORN

Its long limbs allow it to sprint over the sandy desert with bounds of up to **20 feet** (6 m).

Its coat is covered in sharp spines to defend against predators. It has a **four-chambered** stomach, which allows the pronghorn to extract the maximum nutrition from the sparse desert vegetation.

JERBOA

It builds burrows to escape from the extreme daytime heat. Relative to its size, **jerboas** have the largest ears in the animal kingdom. These help to regulate their body heat.

It has a fold of skin that can close off its nostrils to sand and dust.

The jerboa has little need for water. In tests, it has lived off **dry seeds** alone for **three years**.

When threatened, the **Texas horned lizard** can shoot streams of blood from its eye sockets to confuse would-be predators.

The blood can be squirted to a distance of

4 feet (1.2 m),

and contains a foul chemical that's irritating to many enemies.

FENNEC FOX

Its fur-covered paws provide protection against the hot sand.

The fox's long, thick hair keeps it warm during the cold nights and protects it from the hot sun during the day.

Their enormous **4-to-10 inch** (10 to 15 cm) ears release heat from the blood that circulates through them.

Vultures have a unique method of cooling off – they poo on their legs! The moisture from their wee and poo cools the blood in the areas without feathers, which lowers their body temperature.

It's more effective than panting, apparently, but we'll take their word for it!

CHILL OUT

Our next adventure takes us to the chilliest place on Earth, where temperatures can reach a bone-chilling **-144°F** (-98°C).

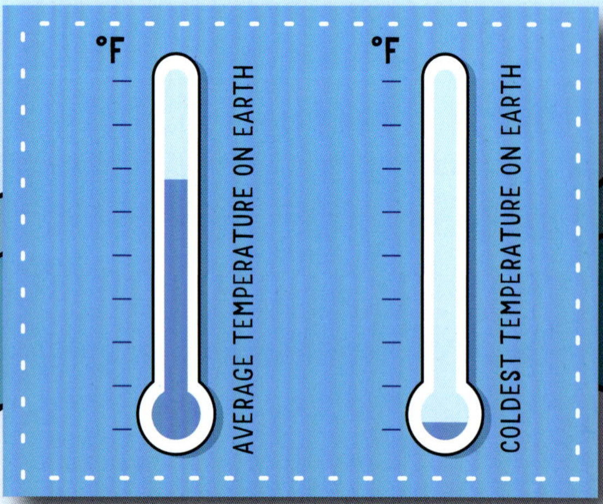

Polar bears are perfectly adapted to survive in the freezing Arctic.

Their thick **double-layered** coat and layer of fat keep them warm, while their snow dens provide protection from the harsh winds. These furry creatures also have a unique way of staying clean: they roll around in snow or take a dip in the icy sea! Brrr!

FREEZING FACT!

Polar bears can weigh up to **1,700 pounds** (771 kg). That's five-times heavier than a panda. When polar bear cubs are born, they're the size of a guinea pig!

Polar bears are great swimmers.

With their large front paws acting as paddles, webbed skin in between their toes and their rear legs held still like a rudder, these creatures can splash through the Arctic waves at **6 miles** (10 km) per hour.

An average polar bear eats **4.4 pounds** (2 kg) of fat each day. They hunt seals and use their terrific sense of smell to track down dead whales, narwhals, or walruses from almost **20 miles** (32 km) away.

A polar bear's stomach can hold up to **20%** of its own body weight.

FURRY FACTS!

Did you know, a polar bear's fur isn't white at all? The hair shafts are actually transparent, which allows the fur to reflect the light of the sun. The see-through hairs direct the sun's rays to the polar bear's black skin, which absorbs the light to provide warmth. Cozy!

The **Arctic hare** is a camouflage champion. It has white hair in the snowy winter and blue-gray fur in summer to blend in with the rocks and vegetation.

The Arctic hare weighs in at **15 pounds** (6.8 kg), or twice the size of a cat.

For warmth, the Arctic hares huddle in groups of **200** and can sprint at **40 miles per hour** (64 km/h) to escape predators. In winter, these animals dig through snow to nibble on woody plants, moss, and lichen.

One way to get warm when you're chilled to the bone is to escape! The **Arctic tern** flies **21,750 miles** (35,000 km) every year to enjoy the Arctic summer for one half of the year and the Antarctic summer for the other half.

That's one of the longest annual migrations of any animal!

With a length of **43 inches** (109 cm)–including its tail–the **Arctic fox** measures just under **four times** the length of a ruler.

They live in burrows and tunnel into the snow during blizzard conditions.

To prevent heat loss, the fox tucks its head and legs under its body and behind its furry tail.

The **Arctic fox** feasts on a variety of foods, including lemmings, voles, sea birds, and even scraps from polar bear kills.

They fatten up in in autumn for insulation during the winter months ahead, sometimes increasing their weight by over **50%**.

Did you know Antarctic-dwelling **Emperor penguins** can be **48 inches** (122 cm) tall? That's taller than a golf club! And they have some pretty awesome ancestors – fossils have shown that mega-penguins from around **37 million years** ago were almost twice as tall. Imagine that!

Emperor penguins keep warm with **two** coats of feathers, a layer of fat, small beaks and flippers to prevent heat loss, and, in the absence of socks, feather-covered legs!

Colonies of **5,000** or more birds bunch together for warmth. But don't worry, everyone takes their turn on the outside where it's cold!

Emperor penguins have a hearty appetite, eating up to **6.6 pounds** (3 kg) of fish and squid every day. This amount **doubles** when they're getting ready for winter.

Record-breaking Emperor penguins have been observed making deep dives of **1,850 feet** (564 m) – the equivalent of six Statues of Liberty stacked on top of each other!

These dives can last an impressive **32 minutes.**

EGG-CELLENT TEAMWORK!

Once the female penguin lays an egg, she leaves! The male partner looks after the unhatched chick for about

65 days,

surviving icy storms, biting winds, and freezing temperatures. He balances the egg on his feet and keeps it warm with a layer of feathery skin called a brood pouch. The female then returns after a couple of months to feed their new addition. What a team!

HIGH ACHIEVERS

Lace up your climbing boots! We're off to discover the mountain-dwelling animals that have a head for heights. Which species have adapted to challenging weather, low oxygen levels, and limited food supply?

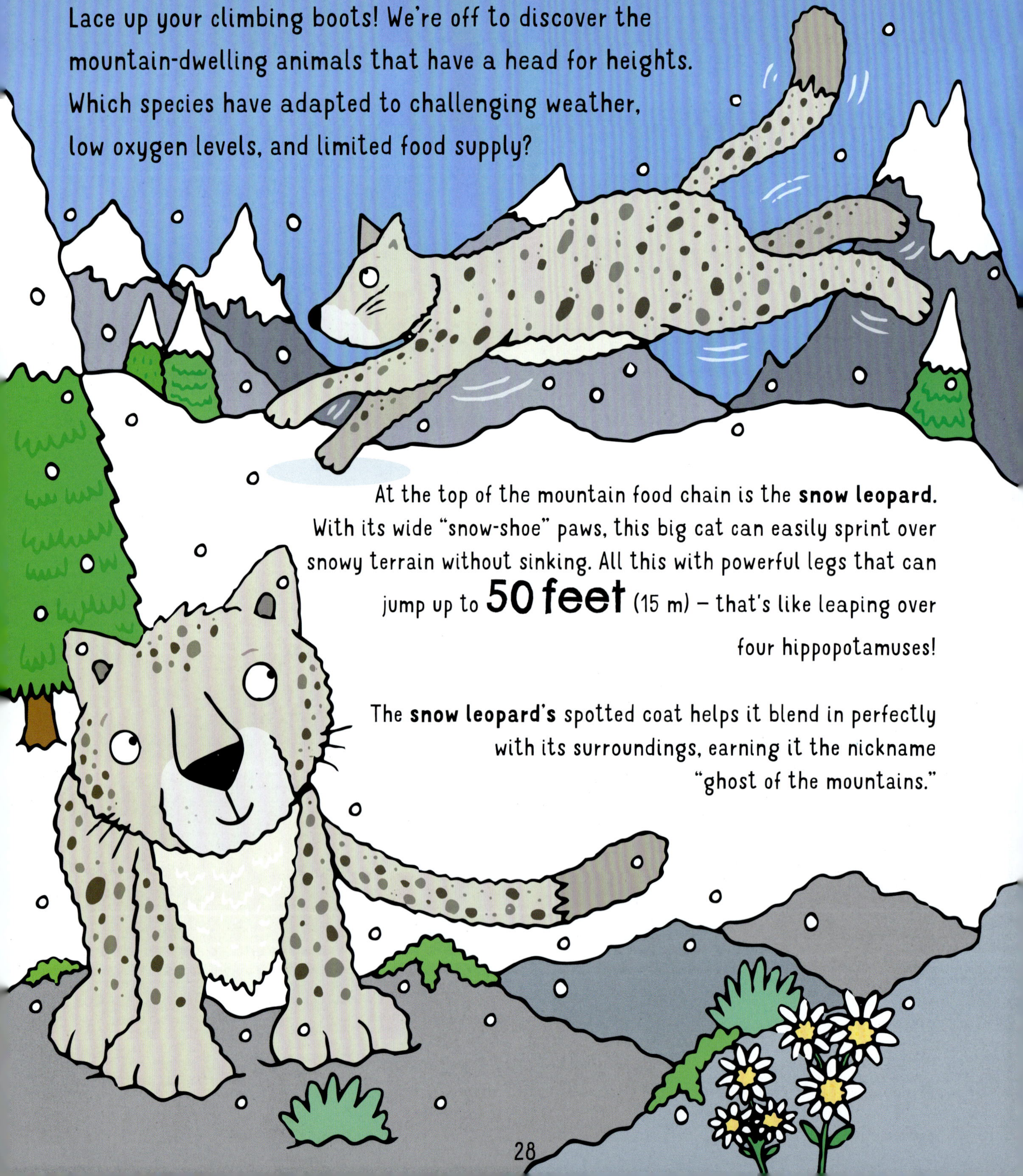

At the top of the mountain food chain is the **snow leopard.** With its wide "snow-shoe" paws, this big cat can easily sprint over snowy terrain without sinking. All this with powerful legs that can jump up to **50 feet** (15 m) – that's like leaping over four hippopotamuses!

The **snow leopard's** spotted coat helps it blend in perfectly with its surroundings, earning it the nickname "ghost of the mountains."

The **golden eagle** is the mountain's speed superstar! When hunting for prey, this top-flight hunter can dive at speeds of over **150 miles per hour** (241 km/h).

When its victim is captured, the golden eagle is unlikely to let go. Its **eight** talons have an incredible grip strength of **500 psi** (which means pounds per square inch, a measurement of pressure). That's strong enough to burst a car tire!

A human has an average grip strength of just **58 psi**!

WOOLLY HEAVYWEIGHTS!

Bighorn sheep are famous for their, well, big horns! The male sheep's horns can weigh up to

52 pounds (23.6 kg)

– that's heavier than all the other bones in his body put together! The horns come in handy when they fight other males, sometimes charging at their opponent at

20 miles per hour (32 km/h).

Fortunately, their thick, bony skull prevents most major injuries!

Have you heard of the amazing **Himalayan tahr?** They are wild goats, found high up in the mountains of China, India, and Nepal.

These adaptable animals have hooves with a rubber-like spongy core, which helps them to grip on to smooth and slippery rocks. Their hooves are lined with a durable material called **keratin.**

Guess what?
Your nails are made of the same stuff!

You'll find **mountain gorillas** on the volcanic slopes of Rwanda, Uganda, and the Democratic Republic of Congo. They live in organized "troops" of around **30** gorillas, led by an older male called a silverback.

If his leadership is challenged, you'd better watch out! The silverback will stand up and roar, hurl things, charge at his opponent, and pound his chest.

The title of champion hibernator belongs to the **Australian Eastern Pygmy Possum.**

This sleepy specimen cozied up for a whopping

367 days!

If you could hibernate, how long would you like to snooze for?

The **Alpine marmot** escapes the cold mountain winters by hibernating for around **200 days,** from the beginning of October until early April.

The marmot family huddle together for warmth, their heart rates lower to **five beats per minute** and their breathing to **one to three breaths per minute** to conserve energy. How clever!

HOME TURF

Let's explore the amazing creatures that call the dry and dusty savannas home. Are you ready to meet some record-breaking animals?

The **giraffe** takes first place as the tallest animal on Earth. It also has one of the longest tongues, measuring a whopping **20 inch** (50 cm)!

Let's see how the giraffe's height compares to that of other animals:

GUESS WHAT!

A giraffe's hooves are as big as dinner plates. One kick from these could really hurt a lion or another unsuspecting predator. Ouch!

The **African elephant** takes first prize for the "Heaviest Land Animal."

The male of this species can weigh up to **7 tons** (6.4 tonnes), which is equivalent to **12½** polar bears!

This impressive creature also boasts the largest ears, teeth, and nose in the animal kingdom!

INCREDIBLE!

Even baby **African elephants** are on the heavier side. A newborn calf weighs in at

265 lb (120 kg),

more than an adult kangaroo! And let's take a moment for the hardworking female African elephant whose pregnancy lasts almost

two years,

making it the longest in the animal kingdom.

When it comes to speed, no other land animal can catch the **cheetah**. This energetic superstar clocks speeds of **70 miles per hour** (114 km/h) and can reach speeds of **60 miles per hour** (97 km/h) from standstill in just **three** strides. Its long legs allow the cheetah to leap more than **23 feet** (7m) in a single move. Wow! That's **three-and-a-half times** the length of your bed!

Check out the top five fastest animals:

Animal	Top speed
1. Cheetah	70.8 mi/h (114 km/h)
2. Ostrich	55.9 mi/h (90 km/h)
3. Pronghorn	55 mi/h (88.5 km/h)
4. Springbok	54.6 mi/h (88 km/h)
5. Quarter horse	54.6 mi/h (88 km/h)

The fastest human is athlete Usain Bolt at a top speed of 27.3 miles per hour (44 km/h).

SPEEDY STATS

The **North American pronghorn** is an incredible long-distance runner, able to maintain a steady speed of **35 miles per hour** (56 km/h) for a few miles. This is thanks to cushioned hooves and efficient oxygen intake.

A word of advice - don't annoy an **ostrich!**

This gigantic bird weighs around **350 pounds** (158 kg) and will tower over you at a height of **9 feet** (2.7m).

It might be flightless, but boy, can this bird run!

It can cover **16 feet** (5 m) in a single stride, holding out its stubby wings for balance. If it does catch you, keep clear of its powerful kick and **4-inch-long** (10 cm) supersharp claws!

The **African wildebeest** holds the top traveling trophy.

Every year, **1.5 million** wildebeest embark on a **500-mile** (800 km) round-trip journey from the Serengeti to the Masai Mara in search of fresh grass.

Along the way, they face challenges such as big cats and crocodile-infested waters. This incredible journey is often called one of the "wonders of the natural world."

GRAB A BITE

It's mealtime! Who are the animals with the biggest appetite? Who are the super-stalkers and the handy hunters? Let's find out!

Lions are the elite hunters of the animal kingdom. Did you know the female lions, called **lionesses**, do most of the hunting for their families? They can run **30%** faster than male lions and have a bite **ten times** stronger than a dog's!

Their supersharp claws can grow to nearly **1.5 inches** (4cm) in length, and a **fifth** front toe acts as a thumb to hold down prey. Lions hunt in packs and use their stealthy stalking skills to catch slower or weaker animals.

WHICH OTHER ANIMALS SHOULD GET A "PREDATOR PRIZE"?

BURMESE PYTHON

Diet	Small mammals and birds. Once, a **5-foot** (1.5 m) alligator was found in a Burmese python's stomach!
Hunting skills	They track their prey using chemical receptors in their tongue and heat sensors along their jaw.
Predator power	Stretchy ligaments in their jaw allow pythons to swallow their food whole!

TIGER

Diet	Wild boar, deer and buffalo. They'll hunt once a week, but can eat up to **90 pounds** (41 kg) of meat in a sitting.
Hunting skills	They hunt alone and at night, patiently stalking their prey before pouncing.
Predator power	Their unique stripe markings act as a camouflage against the long grass and trees.

SALTWATER CROCODILE

Diet	Crabs, turtles, and boar. They eat up to **5 pounds** (2.2 kg) of meat every day.
Hunting skills	They lie in wait beneath the water, with only their eyes and nostrils above the surface.
Predator power	Crocodiles have the strongest bite ever measured. Ouch!

KOMODO DRAGON

Diet	Goats, pigs, deer, and wild boar. A Komodo dragon can eat an extraordinary **80%** of its own body weight in a single meal.
Hunting skills	These reptiles depend on their camouflage, patience, sharp claws, and shark-like teeth.
Predator power	They inject a powerful venom into their prey, then follow the victim for miles until they collapse.

LEOPARD SEAL

Diet	Penguins, birds, fish, and other seals. Their front teeth are sharp and pointed – great for grabbing and tearing.
Hunting skills	They can swim **25 miles per hour** (40 km/h) and make deep dives of up to **250 feet** (76 m) when chasing their prey. That's the same as the wingspan of a jumbo jet!
Predator power	They can skin a penguin by grabbing the bird with their teeth and shaking it powerfully.

GOLDEN EAGLE

Diet	Jack rabbits, prairie dogs, and rodents. On occasion they hunt larger prey too, including deer, bighorn sheep, and seals.
Hunting skills	They use their powerful talons, supersharp eyesight, and flying skills to swoop on unsuspecting prey.
Predator power	The golden eagle can dive at its target at speeds of over **260 miles per hour** (420 km/h).

DUNG DATA

One elephant will produce around **36 tons** of poo every single year. That's as heavy as **50** cows!

Resourceful recyclers have turned this waste into fertilizer, toilet paper, mosquito repellent, coffee, and even award-winning paintings!

The "hungriest bird in the world" award goes to the **hummingbird**, who burns through the calories at speed!

When in flight, the hummingbird's heart pumps away at **1,200 beats per minute**, so it burns a whole lot of energy! You'd have to eat **300** burgers each day to match what this tiny bird gets through in **24** hours!

Who could forget the **African elephant,** the largest land animal on Earth?

It munches on a whopping **330 pounds** (150 kg) of food per day and glugs down **2 gallons** (7.5 l) of water. That's like you eating over a **thousand** bananas a day!

But when it comes to big appetites, nothing beats the **blue whale**.

This ocean-going giant gets through **4 tons** (3.6 mt) of krill every day.
That's the weight of **eight** grand pianos!

That might sound like a lot, but it does have a **200-ton** (180 mt) body to fuel!

Inventive **hippos** have a creative use for their daily **9 pounds** (4 kg) of poop. They mark their territory with **dung middens,** otherwise known as a pile of poo. Male hippos use their tail to flick their poo in all directions to warn off other animals. Yet another reason to avoid an angry hippo!

OUR FURRY FRIENDS

Our animal companions are not only precious pets, they play important roles in our lives too. Let's explore how their acts of bravery and kindness demonstrate their loyalty and affection.

The Dickin Medal was launched in 1943 as a way of rewarding bravery in animals. Since then, **34** dogs, **32** messenger pigeons, **4** horses, and **1** cat have been honored, including:

Sally and Roselle, Labrador guide dogs (awarded in 2011)
For remaining at the side of their blind owners and leading them down **70** floors of the World Trade Center in the September 11 terrorist attack.

Simon, the cat (awarded in 1949)
Simon is the only cat to date to have been awarded the Dickin Medal. Despite being injured in an explosion onboard *HMS Amethyst* during WWII, Simon protected the ship's rations from a rat infestation and raised the morale of the men onboard.

Sergeant Reckless, a carrier horse (awarded in 2016 - posthumously)
Despite being wounded twice, this brave veteran of the Korean War was given the medal for making **51** trips in one day to rescue wounded soldiers from the combat zone.

GI Joe, the pigeon (awarded in 1946)
For making a **20-mile** (32 km) flight in **20** minutes in 1943, carrying a message that saved the lives of **100** Allied soldiers in WWII.

Guide dogs are incredible animals that help those with vision impairment. They are specially trained to guide their owners on routes, locate important objects like bus stops, and even help them to cross busy roads safely.

Search-and-rescue dogs are trained to find missing people after a natural or human-made disaster. They can locate people trapped in rubble after an earthquake or buried under snow almost **16 feet** (5 m) deep. Experts estimate that a single search and rescue dog can accomplish the work of **20 to 30** humans.

Over in Italy, there is an elite group of **350** dogs that make up the Italian School of Water Rescue Dogs. Every year, these brave animals save between **20** and **30** lives. Their rigorous training lasts for **18** months before they move on to more advanced techniques such as jumping from helicopters and leaping from speeding boats.

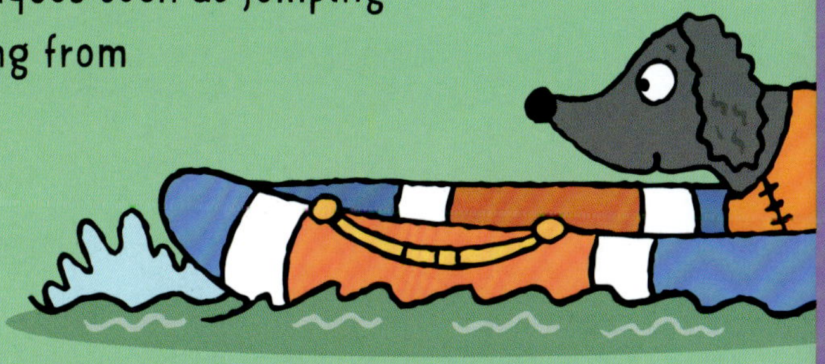

Therapy dogs are specially trained to bring comfort and affection to those in need, often at hospitals, nursing homes, or schools.

SMELLY STATICS

Did you know that your nose has about **five million** olfactory, or smell, receptors?

That's a lot, but dogs have over **200 million** of them!

That's why they make such first-class sniffer dogs, detecting explosives, checking luggage, and searching for missing or stranded people.

Towser the cat was the resident cat at the Glenturret distillery in Scotland.

She can also claim to be the world's greatest mouser, having caught an estimated **28,899** rodents in her lifetime.

In the 1870s, Belgian authorities decided to recruit **37** cats to deliver mail inside waterproof bags attached to their collars. Although the trial run was a partial success, it was thought that a cat's temperament was unreliable, so the plan was put on hold.

Tama the cat was a feline celebrity on the Japanese rail network. In 2007, railway officials honored her with the title of station master and gave her the duty of greeting passengers. Instead of a traditional salary, Tama received a generous supply of cat food for the year, a shiny gold name tag displaying her name and job title, and an adorable station master's hat!

It's thought that the visitors that came to see her added **1.1 billion** yen (the Japanese currency) to the local economy!

Throughout the years, various animals have been sent into space for scientific research, including **mice, cats, frogs, fruit flies, ants, jellyfish,** and **32** monkeys. In 1957, a **dog** named **Laika** became the first animal to orbit Earth on the Russian spacecraft *Sputnik 2.* Laika didn't make it back alive, but her courage opened new possibilities for future space exploration.

PROTECT OUR PLANET

Biodiversity is the name we give to the variety of living things on Earth.

We rely on nature for our necessities – clean water, fresh air, and the food we eat.

Unfortunately, many of Earth's species are facing grave danger. Shockingly, **30%** of mammals are at risk of extinction, with **41,000** species currently under threat.

THE REASONS FOR THIS GLOBAL CRISIS INCLUDE:

- **Changes in our use of the land and sea**
  (e.g. clearing forests to use as farm land)
- **Exploitation of natural resources**
  (e.g. overfishing and mining)
- **The rise of global temperatures**
  (e.g. forcing some animals to move habitats)
- **Pollution**
  (e.g. making land unfit for plant and animal survival)
- **The spread of invasive species**
  (e.g. spreading disease to native animals with no natural immunity)

THESE ANIMALS ARE AT THE GREATEST RISK:

Javan rhinoceros
Amur leopard
Sunda island tiger
Mountain gorilla
Tapanuli orangutan
Yangtze finless porpoise
Black rhinoceros
African forest elephant
Sumatran orangutan
Hawksbill turtle

So, what can we do to make a difference and help protect our planet's biodiversity?

- **You're doing one thing right now!** We all need to educate ourselves about the threat to our natural world.
- You can recycle and reduce waste.
- Make changes to how you get around. Walk, cycle, or use public transportation instead of the car.
- Use less water by taking shorter showers and turning off the tap when you're brushing your teeth.
- Search for recipes that use in-season fruit and vegetables bought from local groceries and farms.
- Plant nectar-producing flowers that will help to preserve the planet's bee population.

TOGETHER, WE CAN MAKE A POSITIVE CHANGE FOR OUR EARTH!

MAKING A COMEBACK!

In 2002, only **15 blue iguanas** remained on the Cayman Islands, and it was one of the most critically endangered reptiles in the world. This distinctive creature was on a one-way track to extinction, due to a combination of building development, human disturbance, traffic, and predators.

Sixteen years later, thanks to a successful breeding program, the **1,000th** blue iguana was released into the wild!

ANIMAL ABC

Check out these helpful words from this book, which you could use when writing about your favorite amazing animals!

Brood pouch
A pocket which protects the eggs of a fish, frog, or penguin

Burrow
A hole or tunnel dug by an animal for shelter

Calf
A young cow, whale, seal, or elephant

Camouflage
A covering or coat which lets an animal or object blend into its surroundings

Colony
A group of animals or birds living closely together

Desert
A dry area of land with few plants and very little rain

Equator
An imaginary line around the middle of the Earth, halfway between the North and South Poles

Fossils
The remains or traces of an ancient animal or plant set in earth or stone

Habitat
The natural environment of a plant or animal

Hibernation
A period of sleep or minimal activity during the winter

Hoof
A hard, tough covering on the feet of animals such as horses and deer

Insulate
To cover an animal or object to reduce heat loss

Keratin
An animal protein found in horns, beaks, hooves, and your nails

Mammal
A warm-blooded animal, with some fur or hair and a skeleton inside its body

Paw
An animal's foot

Predator
An animal that hunts and eats other animals

Prey
An animal that is hunted and eaten by other animals

Rainforest
A dense, wet evergreen forest, usually found in tropical areas

Reptile
A cold-blooded animal, with scales or plates on its skin and a skeleton inside its body

Rodent
A small gnawing mammal with long front teeth, such as a rat or mouse

Savanna
A flat, grass-covered plain

Talon
A bird's claw

Temperature
The measurement of heat or cold

Tundra
A very cold region with little rain and few plants, found near the Arctic Circle

CREATURE QUIZ

Are you up for the Creature Quiz? Let's put your knowledge to the test! The answers can be found at the bottom, but no peeping!

1. How many species of mammals live on our planet?

A. 600 B. 6,000 C. 25,000

2. How long have mammals lived on Earth?

A. 210 million years B. 21 million years

C. 2 million years

3. Which fact is incorrect?

A. All mammals are warm-blooded

B. All mammals have a bony skeleton

C. All mammals lay eggs

D. All mammals breathe air

4. How long can an Emperor penguin dive for?

A. 32 minutes B. 19 minutes

C. 9.5 minutes

5. What are the four rainforest habitats?

A. Top view/Umbrella/Branch line/Mud bath

B. Leaf top/Cover/Middle Earth/Sand dune

C. Emergent/Canopy/Understory/Forest floor

6. How fast would you have to run to keep up with a cheetah?

A. 70 mi/h B. 51 mi/h C. 10 mi/h

7. How much poo does an elephant produce in a single year?

A. 40 tons B. 24 tons

C. 6.6 tons

8. Where is the hottest place on Earth?

A. Gobi Desert B. Karakum Desert

C. Lut Desert

9. What is a camel's hump filled with?

A. Water B. Sand C. Fat

10. What color is a polar bear's fur?

A. Clear B. White C. Black

Answers: 1. B, 2. A, 3. C, 4. A, 5. C, 6. A, 7. A, 8. C, 9. C, 10. A